Animal Babies

Written by Sarah Russell

This is a cow.

How many babies has she got?

A baby cow is a calf.

3

Look at this goat.

How many babies can you see?

A baby goat is a kid.

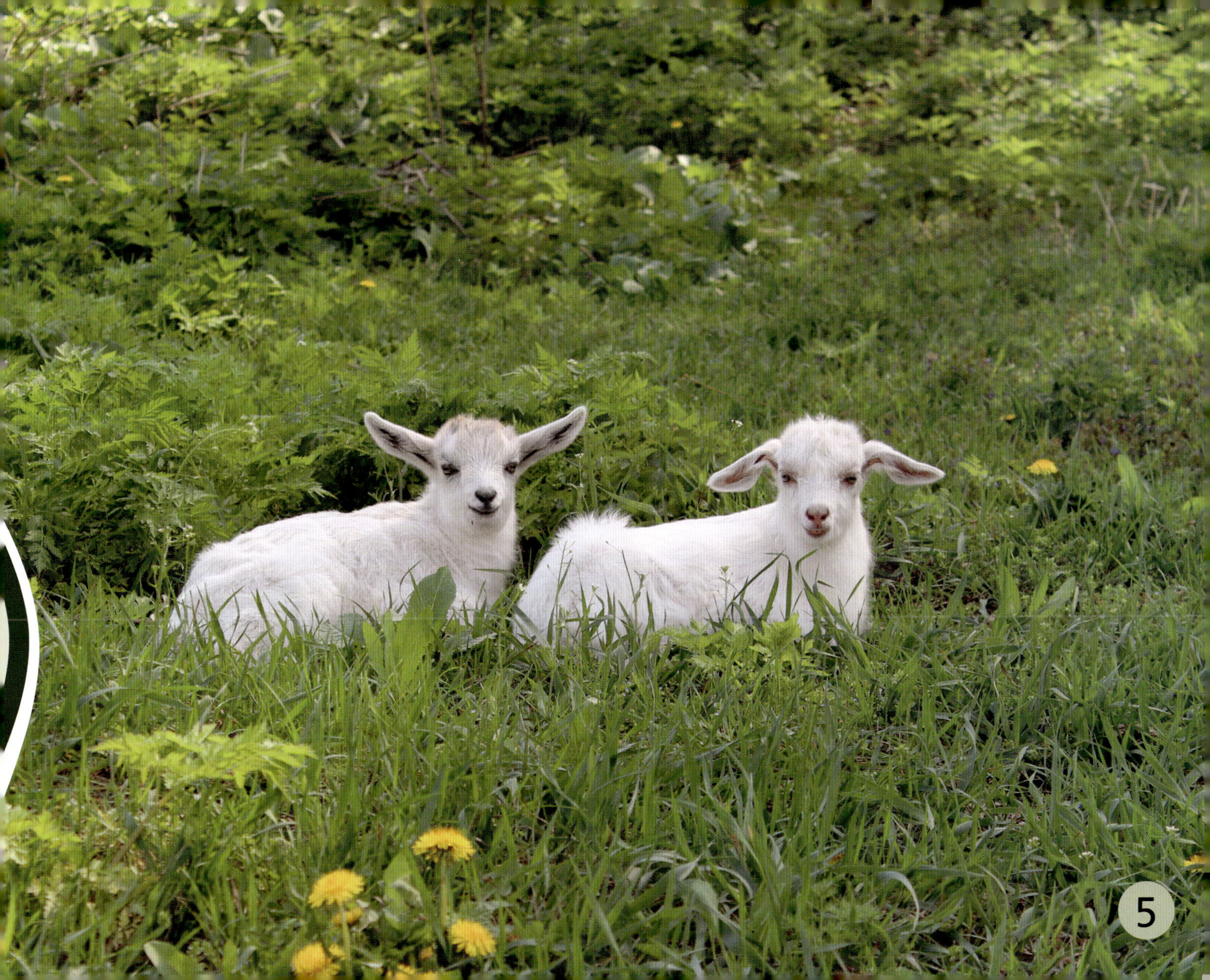

Look at this cat.

How many babies can you see?

A baby cat is a kitten.

7

This is a hen.

How many babies has she got?

A baby hen is a chick.

q

Look at this duck.

How many babies can you see?

A baby duck is a duckling.

Picture Index

calf	2–3	
chick	8–9	
duckling	10–11	
kid	4–5	
kitten	6–7	